DOWN TO
EARTH

BUT NOT BELOW

ROBERT DAWSON

Contents

Down to earth but not below 7

Present and forever 8

Later in the Day 10

Stay in the light 11

Blessed 12

Make it count 13

Existing in peace 14

The hovering tea pots 15

Jump 16

Chaos overload 17

400 degrees 19

2016.AD 20

While I await 21

Brown skin girl 23

Attempt 24

Smile 25

No one will know 26

This is it 27

Light 28

Stiff drink 29

Thoughts while sleeping.............................30

Too much 31

Good to be here......................................32

Closer than you think 33

Winter morning......................................34

Beach moments 35

Be light..36

Beauty...37

Bluish green...38

Sunday breeze 39

Advice...40

The evening...41

All that is good..42

Earth...43

In the now 44

Love..45

Day of light 46

Listening...47

Ninety-eight mph 48

Mine 49

Shift..50

Thinking at 7pm 51

Being cute 53

Altered minds 54

Cali beaches 55

Taking off 56

Just one glass 57

Mans wrong 58

Costly 59

Genius 60

Before evening 61

Color 62

No history is true 63

Brown 64

The struggle 65

Warm 66

Love 67

Fresh air in traffic 68

The broken record 69

Before the light overwhelms 71

Love on Saturdays 72

Present day 73

The glory 74

Earth before 2032 75

Black 77

Blonde 78

Bad ending 79

Light in dark places 80

Love early in the day 82

Lift 83

The king 84

Summer 85

Belief 86

9pm 87

Monday evening 88

DOWN TO EARTH BUT NOT BELOW

This world is not what it seems

Our eyes roam between screens

Then hope and dream about sin

Not knowing what we let in

Wasting the little time we have here

Photos posted then pop up from last year

Memories pile up as we run in a circle

Bruises on bodies, the pain a deep purple

Lies written in books, history a painted picture

Pagan holidays, good times and cold liquor

Agenda of the dark get niggas to hell quicker

Kill love, promote sex and that's the kicker

Christians getting bullied, pastors getting paid

Fingers invoke emotions, nobody runs the fade

Outer space is out of man's control

Lies and CGI, the skies are being patrolled

This world is not what it seems

Without Yeshua it will all end in screams

***

PRESENT AND FOREVER

Faces, I've seen so many faces traveling earth
Wandered from beach-to-beach searching
Does my heart roam the net pondering?
I first met her in my slumber
Completely astounded when I woke up
I've never endured that kind of hunger
Utterly dismayed woke and dumbfounded
This life is nothing I could make up
My dreams touched her origins
So, when we met, we made out
You just couldn't feel it at that time
Soulful black voices singing, I could shout
Ancient Americans danced before the crimes
Yet we still found love centuries of separation
Our ancestors could've been the same tribe
My mind goes out there— I'm enlightened
At ease my heart is at ease
My peace travels with me through seven seas
Above the clouds we hold hands
Knowing tomorrow is God's choice
Man and woman in marriage is God's plan
Who am I to let him down?
Each day a celebration we're above ground

Black love is beautiful, rich and smooth
I hear nothing when I sit above sound
All I see is you

***

LATER IN THE DAY

Black rock in the North Pole
The waters in earth, under control
Anti matter licking its chops to be let in
It's a spooky world with cream and sugar
Nobody sees the danger, just too drunk
Body moving on autopilot it's easy to lose
Winning is narrow in truth
I may not be here when it gets worse
The fallen will take the stage
There is absolutely nothing new under the sun
Are we unaware of what the moon reflects?
Land, I tell you, so much land
This world is not what it seems
In this world, it's safer not to dream
We're headed towards an end
With magic in our hands, pulling focus away
Too high to see what's coming
I'm running towards the light
One will come to astonish with lies
He might even fly and talk a good talk
Don't be fooled don't fold to pressure
Just know it's on the way

***

STAY IN THE LIGHT

Beautiful music, I'm posted by the water

I choose her several times over

Ran into ugly enduring defeat

Life will place bottom into seat

It's better to not be in the streets

I choose her several times over

Been lied too and told stories

Can anyone be perfect in all glory?

Dove deeply in wilderness— it's not for me

I choose her several times over

***

BLESSED

Fireworks sky dance for my dark-hued lover
Your black so beautiful, especially in summer
So rich and swarthy you keep me at awe
You're the most honest soul I ever saw
Like Guinness in class on a Friday afternoon
You look lovely, life is precious under the moon
Earth enraged, its hot in June, you seem fair
I've won and I've lost enough to know rare
Bless the Lord, I found it right here
While everything is falling
Gender roles disappear and so does value
Nothing stays the same, nothing like you
No one compares, life is grand in your presence
Bless the Lord, I found it here

***

MAKE IT COUNT

By the beach, the people laugh

Various colors, some lovers, some searching

The sun blesses till the back burns

Pina coladas and key lime pie

White water makes the heart smile

I'd love to stay here for awhile

The view never gets old, the sea always remains

It's the humans that don't

While blood flows breaths are taken

Live as much as you can

***

EXISTING IN PEACE

Dance slowly under the firmament God created

My desire for you is persuasive

Dread my hair on a weekday evening

I kiss you because I care

Let's brainstorm on what I find intriguing

Tow warm hearts in a world of despair

Dance slowly under the lights God created

Don't let in the anti-matter, lust is destruction

There's a reason there's a wall

Beach with me on a Friday morning

I hold you 'cause I care

Watch from a distance while clouds are forming

So many souls unaware

Dance slowly in the world God created

***

THE HOVERING TEA POTS

I was firmly on the ground

In the forest up and away

Who on earth dreams like this?

Another dimension blew a kiss

They looked like tea pots

Hovering five feet in the air

Take me somewhere show me something

The bodies resting

The mind is hunting

What a tragedy if this dream means nothing

***

JUMP

Stone pyramids in middle America, secret agendas,
    white faces in odd places
We're headed towards the end
The price of eggs will raise brows
We eat so much, they've made fake cows
So distracted these abominations feel allowed
Earth is wild, the entertainers are witches
Young, low-vibration girls sing along
Not knowing what they welcome in
All the adorable things they do are sin
Don't scare me
I've had drinks when I shouldn't
Don't dare me
Fell in love recklessly, I love you now
Don't scare me
I still think I can fly while the world is watching
Don't dare me

***

CHAOS OVERLOAD

The crowd is never quiet

Some love and others hate

Yet they pile up at the gate

Waiting to get in with drink in hand

Welcome to earth, I tell you

It gets wild here,

It's even louder in the dark

The strong will lead

When this system breaks

They are showing the future

Mutations of disgust

Humanity will be judged

When it's too hot just know it's over

I don't ever wanna be stuck here

Nothing compares to Godless life

Please, good words, don't fall on deaf years

Love while the bombs haven't fired

The lies turn into a live action skit

As if the cruel world isn't enough to put up with

Give it to me straight don't mix it

It's already broken you can fix it

Money was too much to manage

War in the cities now here comes the damage

Hiding underground won't save you either
It's coming soon, it's coming
Keep laughing and getting high
Whatever gets you by just know it's coming
To a screeching loud sky-breaking end

***

400 DEGREES

Vibrating higher eyes wide open
I see the danger in the other dimensions
Wars from the past forced religion
I know what belief feels like
History is full of spiteful liars who cater to their lust
Destroying an honest world, distorting things
Ancient Greeks were black and some righteous
They'll curse the sight of you, they never liked us
Civilizations buried underneath stolen land
Fake wars written and taught with bad intent
In a world where they fuck without consent
Shots fire at truth seekers

***

2016.AD

I just wanna hold your hand in the land of Mu
Gazing at all the beauty hidden from us
Eating fresh fruit from wonderful trees
Kissing your cheek, enjoying a cool breeze
Hanging out on a flying machine
They told us didn't exist
The real journey is always accompanied by risk
Don't feel restricted, be yourself around me
I was incomplete when our paths crossed
Orbit my body, I need you all around me
We roam red rocks and walk mountains
Deep convos by the moon
Sun children shine bright in the month of June

***

WHILE I AWAIT

This world is drawing closer to the end
Trumpets will blow
Fires rage throughout the forest
Sink holes all over the earth
They're falling from the sky
With my eyes closed I see it
Laughing all the way to hell
Who knows the future
And what would it feel like
Does anyone experience real life
What does it matter to the blind?
You're all foolish
People are dying while the forest is burning
The aliens shake their heads in disgust
In God we trust the lies we thrust from lips
Sipping on wine while we speak
Follow me on a hill let's watch it burn
Hit the blunt take your time
We don't have much of it
Suffering both rich and poor
Free and captive white and black
Lose family from the wars
Sing joyful songs before it ends

Make friends while you still can

Man has plans that won't work at all

Allow me to lead you to the end

***

BROWN SKIN GIRL

Whose brown eyes and gorgeous undertones
Radiate a shade of black my mind consumes
Kissed by elements sung with no microphone
Running fingers through her fro, inhaling perfume
Atoms exploding in all of my matter
Excitement sprinting through my custom pants
Do hold composer as my cells began to chatter
No music being played my emotions dance
This what Adam must have felt first sight of Eve
to witness you in all your perfection
I'm astounded your ideals fit me like a sleeve
Sun kissed you at the awe of your complexion
The world is ending, maybe not this hour
Sit here in my subconscious with all my power

***

23

ATTEMPT

There's a war above my head
I don't vibrate high enough to see
Tempers flare on earth from sea to sea
Is there any hope for the dead?

I found love while the world was dying
We all long to be hugged and needed
While weary hearts lost yet still competed
Only a few of us get lucky because we're trying

***

SMILE

Who loves the sinner while they sin?

Vodka without a chase

Liars fill the congregation

It's okay for now

Forever is too long to risk

Is it safe to smile?

Love is sacred only when you walk the isle

As we vibrate higher, who can feel the shift?

Yes, it's safe to smile

We're only here for a while — life's a gift

***

NO ONE WILL KNOW

I've pondered on all things
Seen futures through sun shades
Laughed at the scientist
Eyes roll at the screens
Ideas formed after dreams
What a giant world undiscovered
Beings left unbothered
Until the apps started to capture
Drones roam the skies they can't predict time
Nobody will be warned of the rapture
It will just happen
The people will be drunk
Some high and oblivious
Other's shattered from the truth
I've seen visions I can't unsee
None of them are good for y'all
Everything comes to an end

***

THIS IS IT

While the two lights occupy the air

Waves clapping at the beach

Beautiful bodies willing and ready

Shots taken at the bar

How could I wish on a star,

When it's an angel?

Only earth for us

***

LIGHT

Life is lovely bless the Lord
Tell me this is real; I know I'm bonded now
When will it settle in?
Selfies with my teen in the evening
Hours move and I don't like leaving
You take pictures without filters
You're not fragile
Keeping me grounded
I'm astounded we keep elevating
Heights don't seem like heights here
Perception holds nothing
When we embrace, I hold something
I haven't yearned for anything
Absolutely nothing since you came around

***

STIFF DRINK

Magnetic energy beautifully, misbehaving
What have I tapped into?
Sipped wine and seen violence
Lies and mystery fills the earth
No one is leaving ever
Without death, without God, no one is leaving
Rocket ships or nuclear bombs
The firmament ain't breaking
Get closer to God, souls are worth saving
Scream if you have too, run as fast as you can
There is safety in his house
What are we living for, will be worth it in the end
Is mars on earth, passed the ice we can't go to
How do you like your reality?
With a juice or on the rocks?

                              ***

THOUGHTS WHILE SLEEPING

I've questioned the sky more than I should
What truly makes the good book, good?
Pondering on God's will in present day
Moved by faith, I wonder why we can't change
Waters above, not space what's the Milky Way?
I know the truth is never really that strange
Lord knows this is an ugly world
Traveling only where they say we can
Should we fight for the right to choose?
Speak the truth and this life you lose
Deceitful moans on a midnight sky
Sinful kisses taste better when you're high
Everyone's drunk on Friday evening
Driving like nobody is scared to die
What on earth are we doing?
God is not as far as we think
We've been tricked and it hurts
Like a body blow in the 10th round
I'd rather not hear of another planet you found
Knowing you just created it
One lie helps another
We're all in so deep.

***

TOO MUCH

The light reflecting off the firmament blue is
  beautiful
I-love-you-for-a-lifetime kisses on the beach
We've seen a few from time to time
I unwind and think freely
Holding on to the ones that need me
To satisfy the world is a daunting task
Why bother?
Earth is strange and ungodly
Hoping I'm meek enough to inherit
We should only be sharing love
Why does the future look so grim?
Lights dim and music attracts the hearts
Too many moving parts

***

GOOD TO BE HERE

I've seen heights in the islands
Heard stories of past
Roamed past my comfort zone
Sometimes I simply move too fast
This life was made for two
I can't even see myself without her
So, this is what the old people speak of
When you know how old this feels
Each day is worth holding on to
To be under the sun somewhere on a beach
Rum and banana smoothies
Laughter has just begun
Romance under the moon
Dance with me
While the night is still here

***

CLOSER THAN YOU THINK

Beautiful voices sing to me
Wish y'all could hear it
Man, this earth is not the dream they sell
To and fro we sailed always in search of more
Maybe that's what we're fighting for
Lies I've heard from powerful positions
Everyone takes a slice
Oh, how sweet is the money
Why on earth do you keep baking pies?
That kind of hunger can kill you
Who has time to make memories now?
The dollar attracts the girls in thongs
Life created, we fail and make enemies now
We can smoke though
Disobedience is far worse than cancer
It can feel like that for eighteen years that's bull
Sin is disgusting
It gets light with my eyes closed
I get different I'm moving closer
Bold are the predictions
Nothing new was ever invented
Borrowed ideas over the span of centuries
We're headed to the end

***

WINTER MORNING

Nobody falls in love, it's too deep
I'd prefer saying fly
No endless forever going downwards
That's crazy
I wed to you my everything
For a borrowed life I have to give back
Can we have a love made from scratch?
Dancing on ancient tree stumps
You know how I feel about the past
History doesn't show all perspectives
I've neglected practices that raise awareness
I know too much knowledge hurts
I don't think the sun is too far away
Oh my Lord, they're lying
To this world we must detach
Is there better life beyond the ice wall?
Or is there nothing at all?
Everything has meaning
Lord, on your name should we call
I've got more questions I'll leave in mind
Hold my love as we watch
I hear the ignorance all around us
At least they're happy
Not sure they'll be happy when it ends

***

BEACH MOMENTS

Greeted by brown faces I adore this spot

Life on vacation mode

That feels beautiful

Like fresh strawberries with whipped cream

Nine am, isn't she lovely?

I love what the sun does to her skin

Nothing I do to her is a sin

Deep as the Grand Canyon

It's all black — let that sink in

Coconut rum on the beach

As far as the eye can see, I don't see a curve

For all to agree to a lie is absurd

Welcome to earth, people

Two lions chase the herd

My mind can only chase this truth

When I break, my escape is you

If I run, I'm only chasing you

Then I speak and only speak what's true

***

BE LIGHT

To realize fault is growth

Who lies under oath?

God will judge the just too

Knowing the future won't take way right now

Live and love and I in truth love her

Weekdays and winter storms

Fake news and tragedy

On this flat earth with sun worshippers

I choose this hour with you a million times over

Forever in the mind of the beholder

Seas flow and ice chills violently

Misinterpreted scrolls distorted history

A world we barely know

Riots in the hood while the elites drink blood

I'm hand in hand with you always

We're headed to darker times

Be light, my love, be light

***

BEAUTY

Black visions on the beach

Man she's perfect

I hold my rib and sigh

Blessed beyond belief

What a relief, I'm fly

Above and below two hearts in reach

I feel good we found our purpose by chance

Now, tell me who was the target?

Your eyes were shooting arrows

Fixated on forever, rain storms raid the nights in
    June

Ideas dance slowing in tune, I extend light years for
    you

White wine and brown skin on the beaches of
    Beirut

Does forever feel good to you?

***

BLUISH GREEN

The cave people are trippin'
Sun people were born blessed
Stolen land and hidden knowledge
Negros roam the world cold and stressed
The future burns closer like a wild fire at a time
Lighting strikes and rivers runs dry
It's all on our screens web search and see
This is scary in all my earth years I've not seen
Ugly turned righteous are behind the scene
It gets deep like the ocean darker than the cave
Shots fired, inspired by spells that resemble song
Those who walk in the light avoid dark spaces
I've heard stories with bad endings
Sparked the leaf on islands
Unholy things disappear in the light
How can we be in touch
Humanity the repeat of self-destruct
Be in touch internally
The big show is almost here

***

SUNDAY BREEZE

We dance slowly in the evening

Prancing to and fro

Looking at the never changing stars above

Seasons changing the summer is gone

What a summer it was

Memories under the sun

Life takes a different form when you're grounded

It feels good

It's really good, time passes while the slaves work

Dreaming of a better way

This place hooks you like the letter J

Place your feet on grass and meditate

Of all the gorgeous mistakes made by man

War and famine death by hand

***

ADVICE

The living weep for the dead
While all we know is right here
Freedom is what we live for
In reality, free will is what I fear
Anguish in the belly of the sinners
Angels agreed to damn their souls
Lusted as we all did
Only a sharp mind stays in control
Disobedience is the worst pain ever
I've endured heartaches I never had to
Change my beliefs on where we're at
We earth folks are daring, I've got it tattooed
The greatest part of living isn't in what you buy
Time just simply moves so love exclusively
The wrong lover will milk you dry
We only have this lifetime

***

THE EVENING

I like the sky in the Evening
The silence in the trees
Smooth air moonwalking on my shoulder
Another day is done I can breathe
Pondering on the will of God
Grey hairs approach as I'm getting older,
I watch the sky in the evening

We're electric I charge my feet in the grass
Watching planes pass on a flat earth
I found love, I can breathe
In my heart I know God's will
The body doesn't move as quickly
As I watch the sky in the evening

***

ALL THAT IS GOOD

Sitting on the ground above the dirt

Thinking on what I lost

Profoundly painful what we endure on earth

What is each life worth?

Only one way to salvation

Unholy beliefs that will only lead to hurt

We mourn for loved ones

My journey is hard, love while warmth is present

Take words to heart and hug

Be patient with your brothers

Only God will judge in the end

Be still when it thunders

I've wondered why and wandered far

Planted my feet 'cause I'm not getting younger

Cried over the same souls Lord knows I love

My eyes roam the sky in appreciation

All good things come from above

Hold tightly to everything good for you

***

EARTH

Middle of the world or cast out to see

Anger rages through the streets

Lust contaminates the sheets

Lies make the lips sour

No man knows the hour

Be afraid, we should be

It's the believers who rejoice

Doubt can kill you

Don't let it in at all

Drunk nights and regrettable sex

The life of youth in America

Shots fired after two

Check the screens for the update

Behind the screens, who's watching you?

This is crazy —this is right now

Earth, I tell ya

***

IN THE NOW

The earth is flat and sex is free now
The weed is strong as hell
Mixed drinks spiked with drugs
Flooding all around the world
Sick people being slaughtered
Everyone is on their phone
Drones policing from a distance
Lord, I just wanna go home
This is ugly, real ugly
Angry niggas get the Crome
Shooting their way to hell
We as humans will never get along
Liars control everything
Nothing good for you is welcomed
The truth is erased and stories silenced
We're in need of super natural
Gravity doesn't exist, what a myth
The place is wild, it goes down here
During the night, the sinners rage
Saints get ridiculed and told to hush
Bibles getting burned humanity self-destructs

***

LOVE

True love is formed in the mind
Untrustworthy is the heart
It would love anyone in the dark
Our very world needs the light to shine

Real love at times is art
Wild is the imagination of man
It could create lies, misleading hearts
Our very world needs the light

***

DAY OF LIGHT

Ups and downs are a part of this journey
Burning buds only change the state of mind
We've fallen so far from grace
Before reality takes shape
Grab hold of your faith live honestly
Love is rare here, I've cried before
While the drunk make light of sin
Everything is an option for lust
People have searched and found nothing
Absolutely nothing that compares
Over history stories have been shared
Lies written by whites in old books
Paint over brown faces without a care
When the light begins to shine
Nothing in the dark will be spared
On that day

***

LISTENING

Waves clapping as the wind sings its verse

I watch her black body dance

The moon light gliding off her skin

I hear the sirens singing, I just ignore it

The spirits battling above

Our eyes lock and open pathways to the mind

See me for what I am

Naked with all our flaws exposed

God's favor, we exchanged vows

With every decision the afterlife's controlled

So, as we grow older, it's fine

How lovely it will be seeing you in two lifetimes

Right now, it's earth wild as it gets

Laughter and bad jokes, wherever the sun sits

Waves clapping as the wind sings its verse

***

NINETY-EIGHT MPH

Red wine in the evening
Not too much though
I love you bare with your afro
On a plane headed somewhere
My companion, my heart is overwhelmed
Under the greater light
You are the place I call home
Rain dancing in west Africa
Bouncing in America for your love
I'd jump through hoops bending corners
Racing through the jungle at night
Just for you
True love exists in this realm

***

MINE

Beautiful music on an island

You're feet in the ocean's edge

I loved you from the start

We don't have a time limit

This ain't for the faint of heart

Love you more than you can dream of

This is what reality does

Kisses in the evening while the waters speak

I get butterflies during the end of the week

Such a beautiful thing when you find forever

It's my person God gifted

Ad libs and falsetto harmonies

We got everything without a price

What is life?

People ponder on it daily

I don't need to I get it

***

SHIFT

Hiding the truth under dirt and lies

Who prints the books?

The queen is dead, now they're off the hook

Tell the world, say it loud!

Yell from the web, I'll say it proud

Black is beautiful, we were scattered

Dreams shattered in the streets

Heights reached in the middle of the peak

This earth will be for the meek

I hope these few lines find you well

My upbringing led me to preach

The Lord's honor I fully intend to take my seat

Egypt all along the Mississippi

Centuries of lies captivated by colonizers

Wanting what truthfully belongs to me

The world is shifting back to black

***

THINKING AT 7PM

Dancing in the day
Laughter through the smoke
Every leader pushes the button
Fear roams the earth
Man made wild fires succumbing to greed
I'd rather be with you on the beach
You look lovely with your afro
The sun perfects you in the summer
You like red wine before evening
The buzz feels good under the moon
Sweeter than blackberries
Are we in truth what we consume?
Our world is getting crazy
Maybe the end is coming soon
Air. land and sea bold fellows looking to fight
Lies told in crowded rooms
Maybe they are what they consume
We are all given the right to choose
Let's stay right here baby we've got all we need
Together is perfect

The children of Israel fell short
Liars moved continents on the map

The rich profit off the bloodshed
This is earth now as it was in the past
Nothing new here, no progress
People steal and hide the facts
Painting white pictures
In reality Jesus was black
It's all good though
It won't matter when He returns
People of faith will rejoice
All liars will burn
Until then, just relax through the drama
Beach trips with chocolate women
Red wine in the tropics
Laugh while you still can
No matter what's being pushed on the net
Earth will always need a real man
I've got light years of lines I created
Love is all I've ever sought
We're alright here

***

BEING CUTE

To be expressive enough to move mountains

Angelic voices finely sung in tune

My love for you is a fire under the moon

A polite jester you can't refuse

I adore your hair, and Hershey brown lips

Sweet kisses in the middle of a pandemic

Evil people own the media

No man's anger can change God's plan

You were born because I needed you

Dreamt of dancing by the beach while rain falls

As clear as 4k— no brain fog

This is love at a premium with the lights on

Lights everywhere land past the ice wall

We may never get to see it

I'm just glad I get to see you

All we could ask for in a world without promise

Gladly I'll take it

***

ALTERED MINDS

This flat earth is filled with supernatural beings
Liars control the web
Murdering truth for a small fortune
The people are too high to tell
Too high to change dancing with the strange
The alcohol lets the wrong spirit in
Unaware of the danger always something new
The ice above us is blue and we're clueless
I could scream on every channel known to man
Still, they wouldn't hear
Humans are too drunk and high to fear
Too self-absorbed to see the unfortunate reality
We are now at the end
The rich won't be able to buy themselves out
The whites will rage till death
Rightful owners will reclaim the land
Slavery will turn its tide
Oh, what a ride
Fire will eat the unholy far and wide
Underground they attempt to hide
Nowhere is anyone safe here
It's getting wild

***

54

CALI BEACHES

Happiness feels like light on your skin

Move like the waves I love California beaches

Love is gorgeous when it's real

I've seen bright smiles on black faces

Purple kisses in the evening

Each day we're running out of time

I love you completely

Laughter is good for the soul

The atmosphere is smooth in control

Warm hearts heat up this cold world

You always feel like summer

Under the moon light we sip wine

Admiring the journey, we've been at it for awhile

Happiness feels like a cool breeze in the heat

***

TAKING OFF

I needed help and you helped me
Plain and simple
You're rain to my earth
Look what we created
I'm persuasive and so deserving
We look perfect in these light years
If there is such a thing
In a world full of lies we are honest
I wanna be here with the attendance of the sun
We take off on a journey
Someday, past the ice wall, I hope
I have dream-like visions on repeat
So much of earth I'd like to see
You in every setting
I just need you in ever setting
Child-like laughter is good for the soul
found love in a place where the negro was sold
The world is real cold in the December
We only live for what's remembered
All mankind should love like this

***

JUST ONE GLASS

Beautiful ideas, early in my rising
Kickstart my journey with a kiss
I'm the rightful king for all of this
Merlo's dark and bitter
But you're sweet right?
Dance by the waves before we reach night
I've seen glitches in the matrix not surprising

Wonderful experience late in the evening
Light candles, the moon and your shadow
Hold love tightly before Magog goes to battle
Jewelry can be fake and shiny but I'm real
The people clap and cheer for stars that steal
Five shots in the spirits are seething

***

MANS WRONG

Man thinks he's God until he dies

That proves everything doesn't it?

Modify the weather, it's all about control

Earth life is just the start, we go back through skies

Not all of us—that's what scares me

Lord, prepare me, it ain't that fun here

I'm exhausted but I have to be patient

These blood suckers take organs

Tell lies and cover it up

The news is like the blues

Yikes this world is cold as ice in December

Where is the trust here? I wonder what's next

Procreating then separating is a flex

Children grow up unbalanced, lacking discipline

That's who's running the future—if there is one

If there is one, who's telling the story?

This all just a hoax, a huge elaborate joke

Everything is made up

Somebody knows the outcome

We're sprinting in quicksand, an Evil you can't
   outrun

Man thinks he's God until he dies

***

COSTLY

The supernatural: what should we believe

The one came and died and now has the keys

Mystery beneath our feet life gets deep

Like beaches underwater

I'm terrified of this place don't get lost here

Abandoned buildings where the vile did deeds

A room full of liars who all agreed

Whispers in loud places this town is red

Sin just might be the hottest ticket here

Softly touching hearts to change atmosphere

I've wondered why so many chase riches

Neglecting what awaits us is costly

No currency exchange at the gates

Oh, what awaits the souls of man

***

GENIUS

Bright minds are still fickle

Spirits can see who's empty and it's frightening

Leptons and quarks unknown wizardry

Go ahead and add neutrons let's get these atoms
    Poppin'. Silly smart guys opening portals

Being deceived by the dark but much wiser

Relentless beings we don't see in this dimension
    when they walk through it won't be what we
    envision, I see destruction on a mass scale all
    because man has bright ideals

Sad to say you've been used walked on like a
    doormat only to get crushed whether I'm told
    hush or our world self-destructs, it's not going to
    end well, cheer clap your fragile hands, so excited
    for your demise, anguish will ascend upon you

Won't matter how loud you cry, science can't save
    you and money won't matter

Keep burning bibles and worshiping idols

Sale your soul for a few claps and likes on the net
    right now it's all funny and not serious at all

Jokes on you when you're name ain't called
Genius

***

BEFORE EVENING

You must have found me while I was asleep
What dimension were you tapping in
How ever to come so swiftly
Beautiful is your presence
Delightful is you're touch under a southern sky
Louisiana breeze under a pecan tree
Emotions take form and rain dance
Like my ancestors, we have different tribes
The world isn't what it used to be
To and fro, we prance leaving our imprint
In the sand white wine on the beaches
We gain power wherever the sun reaches
I could stay right here forever

**

COLOR

What's the big deal with color, white man?
We built a world you could explore
Played songs to help set the mood
Gave water and handed you food
You ought to be more careful

What's the big deal with color, black man?
A white man built a boat in time of flood
We hate for reasons we feel are just
After the final breath, we return to dust
You ought to be more understanding

***

NO HISTORY IS TRUE

My ancestors roamed America, lived beautifully

White man came and ruined a wet dream

Life is wild but I'm not bitter

Nothing is ever the way it seems

They've changed the Bible hell awaits

The rich get richer and charge for water

Life is harsh but I'm not angry

All sheep unknowingly head to slaughter

I'd like to scream on top of the hill

Watching the world head to the fire

Life is darkness but I'm light here

**

BROWN

Chocolate, I'm all in for your brown skin

Love your hair in the summer

Protect what's held dear to my heart

You look lovely in my dreams

I watch your eyes light up when it thunders

Each breathe you take is art

Now you're here and still feels like a dream

Liberian cocoa kisses on your brown skin

Love your glow in the spring

Held on to the idea from the start

I feel your vibrations when I dream

I kinda like the influence that I'm under

Lifted above the grass we all must play our part

***

THE STRUGGLE

Why is the world ugly?

How much is too much?

Greed is white not black

Like vacuums they suck

All the fun out of this place

Intoxicated beggars by the stores

Too comfortable to face it

Two people ride the bus

There paths are not adjacent

We strive to make enough

Just to get to the beach

Back to work on Monday

History repeats and I'm depleted

This can't go on forever

Nothing on earth lasts that long

***

WARM

I found the real meaning of family

Africa, my wife, her tribe welcomes my blackness

My Ta'merrican blackness, we vibe by the fire

Laughter and red wine aunties dance

While the men talk about the future

This is life, O' Lord, I'm grateful this is life

I've found reality and she's black

She is also love when it rains

Or in the dry heat—what a wonder

The influence I'm under

Fireworks dance in the night sky

Beautiful black people moving to the beat

***

LOVE

T'meri land of love centuries have past

Lies on top of white lies, covered in filth

Riches belong to the ones with bronze feet

History suppressed to stop the rebellion

The truth could change it all

People are waking up

What lies beneath is so hot

It burns forever patiently

The world is too drunk to see it coming

The bright lights excite the brain

It gets wild here, everything is out to get you

Hearts dance with the wild and face the pain

Blue birds sing early morning tunes

I'm pressed over you

Completely, you complete me

Unbothered and underwhelmed by the world

I see you and all your glory

All your imperfections don't mean a thing

***

FRESH AIR IN TRAFFIC

Bright appearance brown skin
Look how well the sun treats you!
Waters wave to you, unbothered and behaved
Hand-crafted over time
How'd you get here in perfect time?
You must have seen me coming
Running through your mind
Fixated on forever, enamored on right now
We've got it right this moon cycle
Watching the world in fits over love
Lacking what money can't buy
Settling for a temporary high
Or a drink they don't need
It's just life here for the lonely
Violins play when I close the door
There is safety in hugs
Passion through eye contact
Supernatural is who I contact
Conversations that bring growth
There's beauty in a dark world
Life is profound by the beach

***

THE BROKEN RECORD

Life started before I could see

Humanity has been fighting for years

For oil and land, kingdoms burn to ash

Liars write books in hopes to turn hero

Blacks being tortured still to this day

Fires rage past the pyramids

We've lost both time and space

We can't retrace the steps

Books hidden in Rome

Honest people get erased

My heart hurts for what has become of earth

Lied to about who's here and where

Maps deceitfully crafted to hide kings

Airships we won't get to fly in

Lipstick on the collars of crooked leaders

Bleeding the poor forgetting God sees all

I grow wearing of knowledge

Endure we must endure a little while longer

The day of the Lord will soon come

No escape for the wicked

There is nothing you can land on the moon

Tragedy in the mind be careful what you consume

Sin dances on the tongue back shots after dark

Too much powder does a number on the heart

Laughter in the streets while the fire heats up

***

BEFORE THE LIGHT OVERWHELMS

Some people will be single for their whole life
Others will chase the high of love
Neglecting salvation, pushing the truth away
I saw you when I was deep in my sleep
You're the dream that never went away
Be careful what song you play on my heart strings
I've noticed forever in your breathe
We gave an oath for the world to see
Hand in hand, follow my steps
We don't know the hour of the Lord
Disaster in every valley of the earth
Blood drenches the streets
Cries heard in the wind, history always repeats
Empires fall, crumbling to the oceans
Secrets only the rich keep
Nothing in this world will matter
After the final night of sleep
I hold you close every chance I get
All we have is each other in this dimension
I know where I'll sit
While the sun and moon split shifts
During the wildness of time
We'll laugh together because right now you're mine

***

LOVE ON SATURDAYS

I still smile when I see her
Voices sing perfectly in tune
Knowing time isn't what they say it is
Can we sit on the beach under the moon?
I've loved you from the start
In the morning, she feels like June
As sweet as blackberries around lunchtime
I guess you are what you consume
I've got hours and hours of affection
Island rum and red kisses on the beach
All of my earth years, I'm hers truly
I will always practice what I preach

***

PRESENT DAY

Blue lips and delayed reactions
Who's responsible for pain?
Why do we cry and yet remain?
Is it going to get uglier
I'm afraid it's getting dark here
People screaming underground
We can't hear them and I can't help them
The disparity of riches is profound
We hate for color, see others and frown
Wondering why we'll never leave the ground
We hope freedom comes but it's not here yet
Lingering through the dark ages of time
Greed is too big to tear down
Disembodied spirts await the willing
Sirens scream from the seas
Man drops nets and make a killing
There's a dollar in every thought
Nothing is being taught in the schools
Lies and pseudo-science gender agenda
Only to work somewhere you don't think is cool
This earth is for the wicked

***

THE GLORY

The glory (Beautifully ascending)

Sing ad libs to the point of change
Vibrating at a frequency high enough to cause
    change, high enough to cure pain
Yah is everything and everything is yah
Your name I dare not take in vain
Man has lied about your whereabouts
Lied about so much, keep me from lies
So, I won't self-destruct, keep me intact
Glued to your words, moved by your word
***

EARTH BEFORE 2032

Scrolling, we keep scrolling, eyes glued

Screens call to you the broken and happy

Feels like someone is always looking at me

I've pondered on forever and it's exhausting

Just hoping we'll be here for it

We haven't evolved, we're diluted

Dumbed down by what we consume

Go get high now that's what people do

Not willing to be sober

Don't mature but grow older

I've drawn conclusions for my own closure

Let me digress, Yah can we grow closer?

This world ain't got nothing for me

Lies covered with chocolate

Angels fell for the beauty of women

Bestowing knowledge for sex

Our true history is so complex

How long do we bare these burdens

All I know for certain is I'm just passing through

I'd rather skip the trans human movement

Sounds scary wild, we think we're in control

In a beautiful mansion, man can be swallowed

    whole by the earth Yah makes a command

The winds listen, obedient is the waters

All truth will be revealed and many will be
    slaughtered when He comes all will see

So much light lighter than any has ever seen no
    need for the real Christ to hide in a dessert let the
    truth reign forever

Can we fathom forever? oh, how beautiful does it
    sound

A world so beautiful, darkness isn't allowed

***

BLACK

You can't undress my black
My hair dreads from blonde to black
Fades then dreads back
My ancestors disobeyed, I inherited pain
War casualties, my people enslaved
Hearts yearning for the truth hidden history
Ask me about native royalty and it's a mystery
Oh, the agony of being robbed
We've screamed for justice in the streets
Centuries have passed yet still hearts throb
Lies covered in white chocolate
Ancient civilizations knew the earth was flat
They tell us we're spinning and insignificant
Only the truth is made from scratch
To what direction does the Great Wall face?
More questions to be silenced
Gunned down if we riot, beaten up if we quit
Only the righteous will win in the end

***

BLONDE

Negro voices harmonizing by the trees
Beautiful melody under the moon
Mother Earth sprays her perfume
I'm enlightened my eyes tracked every hue
Shades of brown everywhere the sun goes
For her does my heart grow fonder by the day
Chocolate and red wine, you're sweet like that
Dragon fruit and black apples, sweet like that
God gets the glory and you're my earthly affection
 fixated on your complexion, I like what I like
You're sweet fresh coconut I drink by the beach
We drink by the beach, slow dancing in the heat
Sun-powered our melanin vibrates on repeat
Days aren't long enough and I won't be blonde
    forever
So, each moment is beautiful

***

BAD ENDING

I wanna see you like right now

Teleport here or fly but come quickly

Breathe in my face, gaze in my brown eyes

I've got centuries of stories I could tell

Danger rages under the streets of Rome

While the dollar wages war on the market

Tell me there is still time for love

Before total blackness and famine

Cell towers burn to ash

In my heart, there is a fire for a lifetime to last

Bathing in the ideas interpreted through moans

Vows repeated, we trust in salvation

Hand in hand, we walk by faith

Watching this world burn to its end

Angels destroy lives, technologically crippled

Those underground bunkers ain't saving a soul

Drunk laughter and disaster stampede the city

I'm on a hill watching the world end

***

LIGHT IN DARK PLACES

Tears, anguish and disgust
We've been robbed for centuries
Our history hidden, this is earth
When will the meek inherit?
The evil women suck and drain
Let no man of free will complain
We're teetering with fire underneath
Laughing while the liquor lets them in
Accompanied by lust skin to skin
Who's really making decisions?
Man has moved past thought and religion
Ushering in a new wave of deceit
Nothing new here, history will repeat
Nothing new here, the niggas face defeat
The sky is blue here, prostitutes offer relief
Witchcraft on the screens while the Bible collets
    dust
Searching for balance while the flesh thirsts
Love scares us, marriage is mutilated by agenda
I couldn't fathom how it felt
The fallen knew there was no forgiveness
Now they're stuck here and they don't like us
Spite in every trick they taught

Lord, only with you should I walk
Where is Egypt? No fly zones in odd places
Sun worshipers create reality on a screen
Sharing things they create, playing God
Will end in flames that never cease
Please don't get stuck here
When it happens: to live in a godless time
Terrifies the woke—don't get caught out there

***

LOVE EARLY IN THE DAY

Hearts in trenched, we've been here for awhile
My heart loves you
So does my mind
Up and away the way you look at me
Gives me everything I need in this life
On this flat surface we surge through valleys
Hiking in the hills, admiring God's work
Tempers at ease kisses that give strength
Nothing is like being here with you
Where does forever begin
Mortal's bargain with time
I'm in touch with energies we dream of
Dancing in my subconscious
I've found what others search the earth for
This is what amazing feels like
Planking long enough to strengthen earth's core
We deserve beautiful earth experiences

***

LIFT

My nigga, there are pyramids everywhere
All around you lift up your head
Ancestor spirits scream
In the waters they bled
Lies, centuries years old, God is all seeing
What is going to happen when He comes?
Everybody's drunk with a blunt in hand
Dancing with devils unaware of what's coming
There's nowhere to run
Sun worshipers will faint
The clueless will be crushed
Earth was never a forever thing
Humanity will self-destruct
Allow me to lead you to the end
Be there waiting and holy
Waiting in truth, it's coming

***

THE KING

From under the dirt of sin,
The prophecy must come forth
Unreal, I've plucked logic from my brain
Normal this was not the agony of the moment
Pain scaled to ten give up the ghost
To give up the ghost
Please don't forsake me, Lord
The only way I could exist
He got up three days later
All over the earth we preach the good news
All hail the king of the Jews
All hail the king of the Jews

Yah would not lie or confuse
Lies told for centuries painters paid off
Covering up the true colors of the holy
Unreal I've plucked logic from my brain
We're now living in revelations
He got up three days later
All hail the black king of the Jews
All hail the black king of the Jews

***

SUMMER

Talk to me like it's summer
Dance on me under the moon in late June
I won't suppress your excitement
You're so beautiful and swarthy
Melanin conversing with the sun
Look what it does to you
I'm captivated
I see frequency dance in tune
This here is electric, you send shockwaves
We are what we consume

Kiss my mouth like it's summer
I speak life to you when the skies pink
Don't hold back what you're feeling
You give life with brilliant color
Melanin slow dancing in the sun
I'm blushing over what it does to you
So captivated
I see frequency dance in tune
This here is electric you send shockwaves
We are what we consume

***

BELIEF

God sits on His throne above the sky
The sun rotates around the stable earth
Lord, please do call me by name
The name you gave to me before birth
Fire eats the Forrest bibles burned down south
Your servants attacked in the holy land
Must I be slow to anger during war?
Can't you see the reach of evil expands?
The angels watch from heaven and I stare back
Time has been stolen, how can we retrieve?
Lord, please do call me by name
Allow me to move mountains I do believe

***

9PM

Kisses before sun starts its race

Light does the body good

Fire cleans better than soap

Sky ice is cold and it floats

The world is more beautiful than you know

Held captive

Why are we held captive?

Man butchered religion, Catholic Mormon or
    baptist

I'd love to see black rock, it's not on the atlas

Few women get married, others are practice

Patience we don't practice, violence we've mastered

Racism is good money, body's get plastered

To disgrace the God above the devil's tantrum

Alcohol lets spirits in, she'll call you handsome

Fornicating after midnight

***

MONDAY EVENING

There's a choir singing down my spine
Native voice's harmonizing with the Negros
I got what I asked for: love is victory
Who on this plain wants drama?
Peace for the beloved: oh, this journey
I grow weary with the torrid pace
Why bother complaining? Keep moving
Work tirelessly until all is taken
You have free will: light or dark
Get your riches now or wait til' later
Only in faith can we see what's greater
There is only one life saver
Yes, yes, my savior
I'm wild and at times reckless
Though I love the creator
Lord, don't forsake me
This world is cold and ugly
Whenever you decide to come
Please take me

***